T0130309

WALKING WITH THE LORD

True Testimony

Dorothy L. Cunningham

Edited by Mary Ann Owens and Lisa Archer

authorHOUSE®

AuthorHouse™
1663 Liberty Drive
Bloomington, IN 47403
www.authorhouse.com
Phone: 1 (800) 839-8640

Scripture quotations marked KJV are from the Holy Bible, King James Version
(Authorized Version). First published in 1611. Quoted from the KJV Classic
Reference Bible, Copyright © 1983 by The Zondervan Corporation.

Published by AuthorHouse 03/24/2015

ISBN: 978-1-5049-0292-2 (sc)
ISBN: 978-1-5049-0293-9 (hc)
ISBN: 978-1-5049-0291-5 (e)

Library of Congress Control Number: 2015904741

Print information available on the last page.

CONTENTS

ACKNOWLEDGEMENT

TO GOD BE THE GLORY

INTRODUCTION

How do I begin? I will begin at the beginning. My father, Thomas Washington Lowrimore, was born in 1904 and grew up in the city of Georgetown, SC. My father's parents had nine children, and he was the eighth. My father's father died in 1918. My father was only 14 years old at the time and his younger brother Lester was 11 years old. This made it hard for the boys to have the right parental guidance. In my book you will see how God moved on my father's life and he became a Christian. My father was a small framed man (5'6" and around 128 lb) but very strong and courageous. My father had hearing loss due to jumping off a bridge. This jump was high and it caused his eardrums to burst. He had little hearing for the rest of his life. Later I will explain how God helped him through his hearing loss.

My mother, Esther Mellie Ellis, was born in 1911 and grew up in the country (Yauhannah section) of Georgetown County,

SC. My mother's parents had seven children, and she was the seventh. My mother had to work hard on the farm milking cows, feeding hogs, cropping tobacco, picking cotton, etc. She and her brothers and sisters had to work very hard, long days. I still remember wonderful stories from my mother and Aunt Mazie (my mother's older sister) about those days on the farm.

My father and mother met through family acquaintance at a social dance in the 1920's. There were few occasions for young people to meet, so usually it was at a social get together. Once they met, it was not long before they fell in love. My grandfather Ellis did not like the young man my mother chose. My grandfather Ellis did not think Thomas was good enough for his daughter because he had a drinking problem. Due to the dislike of my mother's family for my father, my mother and father eloped. They were married on 7-23-1929. My parents had eight children (3 boys and 5 girls) as follows: Thomas Washington Jr. (Buddy), Franklin Calhoun, Hannah Margaret, Marie Esther, Joyce Sarah Jane, Audrey Ann, Dorothy Jane, and Willie Thomas.

My mother was a Christian from a young age. My father didn't become a Christian until later in life. I'm so thankful till this day that they married. We were not rich in material goods, but we were rich in love! It wasn't easy for them during the depression. Their first real home was built by my grandfather Ellis in Yauhannah not far from the home place. After four of their children were born, this house burned down. The children were Buddy (Thomas Jr.), Franklin, Hannah and Marie. My father received a scar on his leg by falling through the floor while saving Hannah from the fire. After my parents' home burned, they moved several times. The time I was told about was when they moved to Georgetown on Front Street and lived in an upstairs apartment. This was the time period when Joyce was born. Later my parents and siblings moved to a shot gun house on Hwy 701. By the time my family were living in the shotgun house (a house that you can see through from the front door to the back door), Audrey was born. She was my parents' sixth child, and she was the first one to be born in a hospital.

These were rough times for my mother. My father was not a Christian, and he made it tough for our family. He was working on the dredge, and he threw away money on alcohol, coming home drunk. His drunkenness forced Momma and my oldest brother Buddy (age 14) to work during World War II. Momma got a job at the I.P. Container Div. and Buddy worked as a mechanic a trade my father knew quite well. Franklin, my second brother, had to babysit my siblings. My sisters Hannah, Marie, Joyce, and Audrey often told me how Franklin took care of them. He built them things to play in and on. I heard about a play house he built for the girls. Franklin also had a goat. He built a cart for the goat to pull. He often gave his sisters a ride in the cart with the goat pulling as he guided. I love to hear the stories of how their big brother cooked and watched after them.

It was during this time my daddy became a Christian. My mother, a Christian, loved him and prayed for him a number of years. One day Daddy came home drunk and wanted Joyce to come hug him hello. Joyce was scared, so she hid behind Momma. Momma told Daddy, "See, you are scaring your children with this drinking and throwing away money that we need for food to feed them." After momma said this to him, he just ran out the house to the woods with his bottle of alcohol in hand. He fell over a log. As he was lying there on the ground, he looked up to the sky. He had a thought to take his life. He was tired of the man he had become. He wanted to be free from alcohol.

My father looked up in the sky again. He started talking to the heavens and said, "I know no one has ever seen your face, God, but if You are real, please change me. I want you to take my life; it's yours." My father then got up and sat on the log. He felt a peace that he had never known. He then got up and looked back to see if Bubba (his nickname) was still sitting there because he felt so new. He was around 43 years old, but he had become a babe in Christ. Thank you, Lord Jesus, for saving my Daddy!

My family made one more move. Due to my grandfather Lowrimore's death, it caused my granny and her two sons to lose their home to back taxes. Many years later my mother through God's guidance was able to get the home place back. My family moved from the shotgun house to the Lowrimore home place. I was told this move was February 2, 1948. Not long after my family moved, Granny came to stay with them. I guess you could say it was Granny's house again. Granny had fallen and broke her hip, and she was in need of help. My father and siblings walked from the shotgun house through the field to their new home. Frank had Marie and Joyce in the cart as he guided the goat, Hannah was walking beside the cart, and Daddy was carrying Audrey on his shoulders. Mother was already there waiting on Daddy and the children to come. When my siblings arrived at the house they were told, "This is your new home. You will never move again." It was true! They never moved again.

My mother took care of Granny, and my family enjoyed her living with them. I have heard so many stories about Granny from my siblings about how much fun she was. She died in January 6, 1950, and I was born February 26, 1950. I never knew her personally, but it seemed like I knew her very well through all the stories I heard. When my siblings talked about her, it reminded me of my father. He loved to make us laugh and do all kind of tricks. He also made us toys to play with and stilts to walk on like in the circus. He even built Willie a go-cart out of an old bicycle and lawnmower motor.

My father was still working on the dredge towing boats in the harbor. I would like to share something my sister Joyce told me after they moved to the home place. When it was time for Daddy to come home from days of work, Joyce said, she would stand on the porch and see Daddy coming down the road with his duffel bag across his shoulder. I am so glad she told me this because my daddy always smoked a pipe, and as she told me I pictured him looking like Popeye the sailor man.

A little while later (not sure of the time), Daddy became a shade-tree mechanic. Don't laugh! He actually had a chain hoist hanging in the big oak tree. He used this to pull motors out of cars and repair them. He had a lot of customers who were appreciative of his work. Much later he did manage to build a garage to work in. I was a teen by then. Daddy worked hard with what he had, and he thanked God often in my presence. See what God can do when He turns a life around. Praise You, Heavenly Father!!!

Willie and I were born after Daddy became a Christian. Daddy could not get enough of the Word (Holy Bible). He loved to read the Bible. Sometimes I would see him reading and tears would come. When we would go to church, I stood beside him. During the singing he would have his arms raised up high and tears flowing down his cheeks. I thought to myself even as a young child, my father looks so happy.

Daddy read Bible stories to Willie and me. Daddy also prayed with Willie and me as we knelt by the bed at night. As I grew older, had homework, and couldn't do prayer time with Daddy and Willie, I always prayed and read my Bible before I fell asleep. I am so glad I was taught to pray and read my Bible. This has helped me grow in the Lord.

Not only was mother full of faith, my father had a strong faith also. I will share their faith at work later. Although Momma loved to sing in church service, she didn't sing to us very much, but my father sure did. I remember many times sitting in the swing on the front porch and him singing to me. He encouraged me to sing in church at a very young age. At age six I was singing "Were You There" all by myself. This was an Easter song. Some of the senior adults would request me to sing even when it wasn't Easter. Together Momma and Daddy taught me so much about the Bible and the way God expected us to live by His Word. This is why my walk with God has been so close all my life. I don't even remember a time not knowing Jesus.

My father was hard of hearing due to him jumping off a tall bridge. His eardrums had burst in both ears. This made it hard for him to hear. When he would go to church service or listen to anyone speak, he would have to hold his ear lobe to hear. His ears bothered him a lot while I was growing up. I saw Momma many times putting warm sweet oil in his ears. I said all this to tell you on Sunday nights as he slept God would reveal to him what the sermons were for that day. On Monday mornings he would tell Momma what he thought was said, and she would confirm and say that's correct.

Just so you know, our family went to church twice on Sunday and every Wednesday night. When it was revival time, it lasted two weeks or more. The more you spend with the Lord, the more you will surely be blessed.

My mother got up really early on Sundays, cooked, got us dressed, and we were on our way to church. Mother just had a determination to be the best she could for the Lord! I love you, Mom and Dad.

My parents did live the rest of their lives at my father's home place, raising us children to know a Living Savior, Jesus Christ, and His Holy Word, the Bible.

I would like to share a little something my parents did for us children, and we did not even know how much love was in it. When mother would cook fried chicken for dinner, my father ate one wing and mother would eat the back bone that had little meat on it. What love they gave their children, the best part of the chicken. Oh yes, my mother never sat with us to eat; she would always wait the table and when we were finished eating, then she would sit and eat.

My father went to heaven on June 6, 1977, and my mother went to heaven on June 12, 1988. At my mother's death, our family had grown to 101 people. Due to the lives that my parents lived before me, they taught me so much about the Lord, as you will see in the upcoming chapters. TO GOD BE THE GLORY!

THANK YOU: To my two sisters, Joyce Sarah Jane Lowrimore Huey, Audrey Ann Lowrimore Watson and my brother Franklin Calhoun Lowrimore, for their help in memories before I was born.

My family- Daddy, Audrey, Frank, Hannah, Joyce and Marie on their way
to Granny's house through the field. February 2, 1948

Momma waiting on steps at Granny's home

My mother and me, age 3

My father and me, age 2

Family Picture, Easter 1965:

From Left to Right - Audrey, Joyce, Franklin, Daddy,

Momma, Buddy, Willie, Dorothy (me), Hannah and Marie

CHAPTER ONE

FIVE YEARS OLD

I was five years old when I had my first prayer answered. This was even before I knew Him as my personal Savior. God is awesome!

My father's youngest brother was always special to me. His name was Lester. I had a special kind of love for him. He was a fisherman, and he would tell me stories about his adventures. Uncle Lester showed me turtle eggs, shells, and conks he found while fishing. Everything he would tell me was so exciting. Uncle Lester even had a crooked finger on his right hand. He received this injury from a fin of a fish. I don't remember what kind of fish, but he did tell me so.

Uncle Lester lived in a school bus that was parked in our side yard. This bus was parked near the big oak tree. He had a bus seat sitting outside the bus where he would sit most of the time. Uncle Lester would build fires near the seat to cook his seafood. He did have a little stove inside the bus, but a lot of times he cooked outside. He always wore khaki shirts and pants. His hair seemed to stick up all over most of the time, and he smelled bad. The smell never bother me. When he would go out fishing, he would be gone for days or even weeks. It seemed like a very long time to a five year old. When he came back, I could not wait to see what he had brought home from the sea. One day he had a fire going outside on the ground in front of his bus. Uncle Lester called for me, "Dorothy, come here. I want to show you how to cook turtle eggs." I started to run towards him. My mother called me back. I could hear him say, "Oh Esther, let her come." Momma would say to me, "Not right now. Maybe later." I started to cry, "Why, Momma?" She would whisper, "Uncle Lester is sick right now." I started crying and ran to the porch as fast as I could.

I didn't know at five years old that my Uncle Lester had a drinking problem. I guess my dad and Uncle Lester grew up too fast too young. They both were young when my grandfather died. My daddy was already a Christian when I was born and he did not allow drinking in our home, so I knew nothing about alcohol or the smell of it. My mother would always keep me from Uncle Lester when he was in a bad way. She never said he was drunk. She would say, "He is sick," or "You can't go right now."

Uncle Lester called for me another time, and Mother would not let me go again. I just knew in my heart Uncle Lester would be sad if I didn't come, so it made me upset. I went to the swing on the front porch, peeping at him through the slats. His home in the bus was right there where I could see him sitting with his fire and cooking. I started to cry because my heart was broken. I didn't know the real reason mother didn't want me to go. As a child of five, I thought it was because he was dirty, with his hair sticking up, and he smelled bad. From the bottom of my heart, I could feel the hurt so deep. I kept crying out to Jesus. You see, I had heard that Name above all names many times. I cried, "J-E-S-U-S, please let Uncle Lester wear a suit so I can go see him." I didn't know how to pray for his salvation because I did not have the understanding at age five. Many times after that I prayed for him to wear a suit.

A few years later Uncle Lester left our home place. His bus was moved. I was told he lived on a houseboat behind the fire station on Front Street. He also became the captain of a yacht for a very rich man. I missed him very much, but I never forgot him.

I always looked forward to his visits. Uncle Lester often came by to visit Daddy and us. I remember one special visit when I was about twelve years old. He drove up in a nice big car, his hair was combed so nice and he was wearing a suit! My eyes opened so big. The Good Lord quickly reminded me of all the times I had prayed for him to wear a suit when I was really young. In my heart, while I was smiling, I was thanking God so much for answering my prayer. I said to him, "Oh Uncle Lester, you look so handsome. God has really blessed you." He said to me, "God nothing! I did it myself. I go to AA with friends." My heart sank because I was not used to anyone speaking about God in that tone. I thought to myself, I need to pray for his salvation in a hurry!

Uncle Lester had a reason for coming by. He wanted me to ride with him to Aunt Lavenia's house. She was Uncle Lester and

Daddy's older sister. Her home was far out in the country. Uncle Lester said, "Esther, I would like Dorothy to ride with me to Lavenia's." Mother said no to Uncle Lester. I said, "Please, Please, let me go." Uncle Lester said, "Dorothy will be fine, Esther. I will take good care of her." Of course, I said please again. Momma, against her wishes, let me go. I had a great time with my Uncle Lester. My dad and Uncle Lester were so different, yet I noticed they both like to sing. We sang all the way to my aunt's house and back. Many times after the first trip Uncle Lester would come by to ask me to ride with him again. When we were on the road, he would ask, "What is the song that says walk with the Lord?" I would say, "Just A Closer Walk." Then we would begin singing. I believe he loved that song the best. Uncle Lester lived until his eighties. Most every time I would see Uncle Lester from then on he was wearing a suit.

I do believe he did come to know the Lord in his old age. His conversation about the Lord was different. When I had the opportunity, I would talk to him about the Lord. He told me about a preacher who gave him the Bible on cassette tapes. (You see, Uncle Lester could not read or write. My daddy told me he cut school to go fishing, although he did learn to write his name.) Uncle Lester told me he enjoyed listening to the tapes. Uncle Lester had no chance to hear the Word until this wonderful preacher came into his life. It's another story, but this preacher was from Louisiana, and he met Uncle Lester while he was working on a dredge boat in the Winyah Bay. I met Brother Earl (same preacher and this is what I called him) in a church service around the same time not knowing he was the one who gave Uncle Lester the Bible on tapes. It was years later beside Brother Earl's death bed in Louisiana that I learned he knew Uncle Lester. Brother Earl asked about uncle Lester. I said, "you're the one who gave him the tapes!" He said yes. Isn't God good? He sent a man who was full of faith to my uncle, for whom I had been praying for so long. In my adult years, Brother Earl helped me grow too. Like I said, that is another story in itself.

The Good Lord answered my prayers at five years old, and He answered many more through my life.

Uncle Lester with turtle eggs.

Please Jesus give Uncle Lester a suit so I can visit him.

Uncle Lester with his new car and suit.

CHAPTER TWO

SEVEN YEARS OLD

While I was seven through eleven, there were no special prayers answered for me alone, but this was a time in my life when prayers were answered for others that I felt deep in my soul.

It was a natural thing for my father to read a Bible story and Bible verses at night before we went to bed. My father, Willie, and me knelt beside our bed to say our prayers before going to sleep. Even in the day time when one of us got hurt, we would kneel and take it to the Lord in prayer. My mother and father definitely believed in the power of prayer.

MOTHER'S FAITH: My mother lived the life of a peacemaker. My sister Joyce described her as the "Silent Strength." No matter how long it took for a prayer to be answered, she kept the faith.

My two oldest brothers, Buddy and Franklin, were both married by the time I was two years old. I don't remember anything at all during that time. I would like to share a memory when I was seven. I was wakened in the middle of the night hearing someone crying. You see, this is when my mother with her burdened heart went to the Lord in prayer. Mother would wake up and have a burden for her sons and cry unto the Lord. I remember peeping out the bedroom door and seeing Momma kneeling at the couch calling their names out in prayer. "Oh Father, please save my boys. Please bring them home safely." I could hear a sound come from her like mmmmmmmmmmmm, a sorrowful sound. Mother interceded for her children more often than I even know. God did answer her prayers. I don't know the exact timing, but just as Momma prayed for Daddy for years, it also happened for Franklin. Buddy's salvation didn't come until he was old.

We were in revival at church, and Franklin came to the revival. The Lord was dealing with his heart. My sister Joyce went to him and told him she would go with him to the altar. Franklin became a Christian that night. I was so happy for him. I remember the joyful feeling so well. Franklin changed forever. He didn't mess

9

around with his old buddies anymore but when he saw them, he would tell them about Jesus. They would laugh at him and say, "You'll be right back with us before too long."

When the Lord saved Franklin, He made him new. It wasn't long after he became a new creature in Christ, the Lord called him to preach. God blessed Frank with a ministry where many souls were saved. He also had another calling on his life. He built church houses for the Lord from the ground up. I believe God was preparing Frank all along. You see, he built structures (cart, playhouses, etc.) even as a child. The first church house in his ministry is the one in which I was saved. There were three more churches God used him in developing and building from the ground up. This is really a story he needs to tell. God blessed him so greatly. I couldn't explain with the honor it needs. Thank you, Lord, for Franklin and his inspiration in my life.

There is something else I remember about my mother faith. When she cooked at lunch time during the week and on Sundays, she fed many. I can remember going to her house on Sundays after morning worship eating and again on Sunday nights and her pots would still be full. One day I said to her,

"Momma your pots seem to always be full. I can cook for my little family and we empty my pots." She said to me "Dorothy, I have always asked God to bless my pots so I could feed those that come." God is awesome!

FATHER'S FAITH: I noticed when my father prayed, he believed as soon as he asked. It was never a question will God answer but thanking Him for the answer.

I remember when I was eleven years old the church that my brother Frank and another pastor had started was in its third year. We were having Vacation Bible School in the morning hours during the summer time. It was during lunch time when all the children went outside to eat and play. One of the older boys (Bobby) had a bicycle he was riding and chasing the smaller children. He was told several times to stop, but he didn't listen. My younger brother Willie (6 years old) was running around the back corner of the church. Bobby sped up and ran over Willie's leg. Both bones were broken and sticking out the side of his little, scrawny leg. My mother just about fainted at the sight of it. I actually did not see it because Momma would not let me. Willie and Momma were rushed to the hospital by my sister Joyce (Thank God she was visiting us; she was so helpful.) Like I told you earlier, my father was a shade-tree mechanic, and he was working at the time this happened. My father was told about the accident by my sister Joyce, so he rushed to the hospital as fast as he could, grease and all. When he arrived, he saw Momma crying. She said, "Oh Daddy, Willie has to have an operation." Momma said, "I was told that we need $125.00 before they will operate. Willie has to have pins in his leg. It's a serious operation." After seeing Willie in the emergency room, Daddy told Momma to tell the doctor to go ahead with the operation. Momma said, "But we don't have the money." Daddy said, "God will provide." He said, "Esther, I'm going home to clean up and I'll be right back." Momma was still worried about the money. Daddy could see it in her eyes that she was worried, so again he told her, "God will provide! Tell the doctor to schedule the operation, and I will bring the money back before they start." Times were tough for our family with no insurance, but God did provide.

On his way home to clean up, my father stopped at a gas station to get gas. One of his customers (car repair) walked up to him and said, "Mr. Lowrimore, here is the rest of the money

I owe you. I'm sorry I didn't come by to pay you, but I'm glad I saw you." Daddy told him, "Thank you. I would talk to you longer, but I am in a hurry to get back to the hospital because my son is going to be operated on." Daddy drove up in the yard and ran in the house to get ready. While Daddy was getting ready, a knock was at the door. Daddy opened the door and it was another customer who owed him money. The customer said, "I remembered that I owed you this money. I'm so sorry it's late." Daddy said, "Thank you. It's okay." (Daddy had a lot of customers who loved his work, but they didn't pay all at once. Daddy would say everyone is having it hard; when you get the money come pay me.) After his bath, Daddy started back to the hospital. He knew he didn't quite have enough money, but he kept on his journey back to the hospital. You see, he knew God would provide. As Daddy was driving on Hwy 521, he saw a car stopped on the side of the road. (Daddy often stopped to help people on the side of the road with no thought of repayment. That was the kind of person he was, to help where he was needed even when he was in need himself.) Daddy started not to stop because he was in a hurry, but something inside said turn around and help them. Daddy turned his car around and went back to the people on the side of the road. It didn't take him long to fix the car so they could be on their way again. The owner of the car handed him some money. Daddy said, "That's okay. I was glad to help." The man did not take that for an answer; he said, "I want you to take this money. I was just traveling through your town and my car stopped. I would still be sitting here for a long time if you hadn't stopped to help me. I want you to have this money." He handed the money to Daddy rolled up, and Daddy stuck it in his pocket. Daddy thanked the man and never looked at the money until he got to the hospital. When he saw Momma, Daddy pulled the money out and started to count. He had the $125.00 plus some. He looked at Momma and said, "Esther God did provide." I heard Daddy tell his testimony in church. Daddy just asked and he knew he would receive. Worry was not in his vocabulary. "Thank you, Lord, for a father full of faith in You."

Something else occurred when I was seven. This was Christmas time in 1957. I never got too much at Christmas like children do today. I would get a doll, a dress, fruit, and nuts. The Christmas of 1957 was different. I received so much I felt unworthy. Yes, even at seven I felt I didn't deserve all what I got. I got a dress, doll, tea-set, iron, ironing board, and a real baby carriage that would hold a live baby. I was so happy in my heart about all my gifts, I couldn't help myself. I was thanking God all morning.

After breakfast, I went outside to stroll my baby doll in the carriage. As I was walking and looking up in the sky, thanking God with every step, I thought of something I heard in church about His coming again. I said, "Thank You, Lord Jesus, for coming to get us!!!" All my life, on and off, I have thought about that moment when I looked up. Even to this day I feel I will see Him come back again. I am 65 years old now, and I have seen this world go from hardly any electronics to everything is computer and electronics. Food is ten times higher than it was. Gas was only 23 cents a gallon, Pepsi 8 cents, and poor boy cake 3 cents, when I was a teenager. Worst of all, the world has gotten wicked. Jesus and what He did on the cross is left out. This makes me so sad. In my opinion Churches are not letting the Holy Spirit lead services.

I know He is coming again. Thank you, Lord Jesus, for your saving Grace. I LOOK FORWARD TO YOU COMING!!!

Momma praying for her children

I was awaken by Momma crying

CHAPTER THREE

THIRTEEN YEARS OLD

Ages nine through thirteen were a growing time for me. I sang specials in church often. My father would ask me to sing "I Surrender All" with him as a special. At the age of thirteen is when I really met the Master. I will tell you later in this chapter. Before I do, I want to share some memories that taught me lessons.

I would like to share how my father and mother helped people get to church service. I think about it now, and I don't know how it worked except by the grace of God. In the 60's there were no seat belt laws. Thank God for that because what I'm about to tell you is true but hard to believe. Of course my sisters Hannah (1955), Marie (1959), and Joyce (1960) were married, but three of us children were still left at home (Audrey, me, and Willie). There were two families (Walkers and Chestnuts) that wanted to come to church but did not have a vehicle or any other way to come. My father told them he would pick them up for church service. My father had an old four-door Ford. (Today I have a Mercury Marques, and there is no way it would hold the crowd.) On the front seat Daddy would be driving, with Willie standing between Daddy and Momma. I would be sitting on the edge of seat between Momma and Mrs. Chestnut. Mrs. Chestnut was blind but very talented. She played an accordion and piano. She and Mr. Chestnut sang specials, and later she became our pianist. When Mrs. Chestnut's daughter came to church, she would sit on the edge of the seat, and I would sit on Momma's knees. On the back seat would be Mr. Chestnut, Mr. Walker, and Mrs. Walker. Audrey would sit on the edge of the seat between two of the grownups. Mr. and Mrs. Walker's daughter Linda would sit on Mr. Walker's knee. Sometimes the Walkers' two older daughters would come also. They also had an edge or a knee to sit on. Through my life as a child, this would be our trip to church Sunday morning, Sunday night, and Wednesdays. There was always good conversation, laughter, and singing as we traveled to church.

Tire Trouble: What was funny (or maybe something to be thankful for), sometimes when we pulled up in the church yard, one of the tires would go flat. Daddy would laugh and thank God that we made it and would change the tire. Daddy would always be thankful it didn't happen on the road but waited until we stopped. You see, he had different sizes of tires in the trunk of his car so he could help himself or travelers he met on the road. Daddy seemed to always be prepared. I even remember pulling up in the yard at home, and a few minutes later a tire would go flat. I would hear daddy say, "Thank You, Lord, we made it home and I have a spare." You see, a person like my father had to really love the Lord to take on a responsibility like he had. I never heard him complain. By his Christian walk, I was taught to do unto others as you would have them do to you. Thank You, Lord Jesus.

Our church was really growing, and we had a number of young people attending. You could really feel the spirit of the Lord (His Presence) in our services. A number of souls came to the Lord, and lives were changed. When we were in church services, I always had to sit with my family. My mother was always strict while I was growing up. Daddy left all the punishment up to her, if need be. As I got older, she did allow me to sit on the second row across from her with other young people.

MY SALVATION: Our church was in revival. I would say that back in the 50's and 60's we really had revival two weeks or more. Churches these days are really missing out on the power of God.

On Sunday night during the second week of revival, I was sitting on the second row with friends. I was thirteen at the time. We had already had such a wonderful service in the Lord with singing, specials, and testimonies. Franklin was preaching a sermon about how people try to travel different ways to get to heaven, but there was only one way: JESUS AND WHAT HE DID AT THE CROSS. After the sermon was over and the music started, my heart was pounding. The song that was being sung was "Have Thine Own Way, Lord." We had sung this song many times before, but I never felt this. I always knew about Jesus and His Love. I was taught this from a youth up. What was I feeling? My heart started to throb faster. People were going to the altar and weeping. I had seen this many times and always rejoiced with them. The song had already been sung once and started over. I was singing, but my heart was pounding so hard I felt it in my throat. I heard Franklin say, "The Lord is knocking at your heart's door; come to Him." I put my song book down because

I knew the song by heart anyway. I placed my hands firmly on the seat in front of me. I was talking to God in my mind. I said, "I don't know what has happened, but if I go up there people will think I'm bad. I have always obeyed my parents, sang for You, Lord, and was happy to do so." I looked over at Momma and Daddy, and something spoke inside me (I didn't actually hear words, but I heard it in my heart.) He said, "I have no grandchildren." I answered, "I know now, Lord Jesus, I have to do this myself. I can't go to heaven on Momma's and Daddy's walk with You." The song was finishing up for the second time. I said, "Oh no, Lord Jesus, they have stopped." I started to cry with a deep cry, it's too late (it makes me cry even as I am typing this). I said, "Please, Lord Jesus, let them sing again." About the same time I heard Franklin say, "Sing it again. There are more that need to come." I took the first step and the Lord took over. I repented of my sins and asked Him to come in my heart. "Please, Lord Jesus, let Your light shine through my life; it's yours." We are all sinners saved by grace and not ourselves. Even though I knew about Him, it was different when I knew Him for real. I felt His presence in my life the moment I gave Him my life. I realized then how important it was for all my friends and family to know Him as their personal Savior. I became an interceder for many souls and still am in my old age. I have always enjoyed talking to God in the name of Jesus. He's my best friend.

The night I became a Christian there were fourteen young people saved (accepted the Lord Jesus as their personal savior). After about two weeks on a Sunday afternoon, we had a baptizing at Black River. As we were singing "Shall We Gather at the River," there were around twenty (I can't remember correct total) people baptized. Even the baptizing was a wonderful experience for me. I felt His presence so strong as I came up out the water. The only word to describe His Glory is "HALLELUJAH." "WE SERVE AN AWESOME GOD!" "THANK YOU LORD JESUS FOR YOUR SAVING GRACE!"

I really had a hunger to read the Bible and pray without ceasing. I realized that the Holy Spirit was guiding me when I saw the scriptures after I experienced the hunger. It was like a confirmation. Matthew 5:6 "Blessed are they which do hunger and thirst after righteousness: for they shall be filled" and I Thessalonians 5:17 "Pray without ceasing." I've always asked the good Lord to lead and guide my life and He has.

This is just an example what went on when I first became a Christian.

There are so many blessings I could share. I feel that I must share one prayer blessing that started when I was fifteen and ended when I was forty five. It was this time in my life I started singing a particular song: "Sorry I Never Knew You" (about a man having a dream of the end times). I did sing other songs, but this one song many people remembered. When I would go to other churches, I would have a request to sing "Sorry I Never Knew You." When I would get to the third verse of this song, I would always think of Buddy (my oldest brother).

Buddy was not a Christian and he would not go to church but his children would sometimes go with us to church. As I would sing, I would look at the audience, see his children, and weep inside to where I would lose my place in the third verse. For years Buddy was encouraged to go to church, and he would not go. He was prayed for by me and many of my family members. My mother once told me that Buddy would have it hard to go under, around, and over her prayers. I always hoped he would come to worship so I could sing this song to him. I felt God gave me this song for him. On several occasions I tried to talk to Buddy about turning his life over to the Lord Jesus, but he would just say, "Jesus and I have a good thing going." In my heart I knew it was not so.

Later in life Buddy was in and out the hospital for a long period of time. Buddy was soon moved to a Health Care Center because he didn't have long to live. I became so worried about him. I went to Franklin (my brother who is a preacher). I told Franklin I was concerned about Buddy's salvation. Franklin told me he had prayer with him and read scripture to Buddy. He believed Buddy was alright with the Lord.

Franklin did tell me he was going to have service at the medical center where Buddy was a patient. The services were held on Sunday evenings. Franklin asked me to help with the singing, so I told him I would. Buddy seemed so happy to see us there having services. He got so busy in his wheel chair going to different rooms telling everyone to come to service that he wasn't listening to the songs and preaching himself. All I could do was pray inside, "Jesus, please let him hear the song. One of the services he did make it back in time to hear "Sorry I Never

Knew You." I had to miss the next week of service. The second week after Buddy hearing the song, Frank asked, "Is there anyone who would like to request a song?" Buddy said, "I would like for Dorothy to sing the dream song." My heart leaped with joy. I knew then God had spoken to him since I last saw him. I sang it one more time for him. Buddy died early on the Thursday morning (October 5, 1995) shortly after that particular Sunday service. Willie, my youngest brother, called me and said Buddy had passed. I felt a peace that was indescribable. I told Willie, "I don't understand. I was so worried about Buddy, but I feel peace." Willie said, "Buddy must be at rest because I felt the same peace as you did when I heard." I still didn't understand and I kept asking God for the understanding. Buddy's funeral was that same week, but Franklin decided to have service on Sunday evening anyway for the other patients. Before services started, my brothers were taking the equipment in and I was following with song books. As I entered the door, a nurse asked me was I with the Lowrimore family. I said yes. She said, "I have something I need to tell you about Mr. Lowrimore." I said, "Are you talking about Buddy my brother?" The nurse said yes. She continued telling me she was on duty Tuesday night and Mr. Lowrimore wanted a cigarette. The nurse said, "I knew he was too weak, but he insisted. I helped him in a wheel chair, rolled him outside, and lit his cigarette. All of a sudden he threw the cigarette down, put his arms in the air, and started crying out to God." The nurse told me that she was a Catholic and that she shouldn't have stayed to hear him but he was too weak for her to leave him. I said to the nurse, "What did he say?" She said, he said, "Oh Father please forgive me; I have not served you; I have not been a good husband or father; I have wasted my life; please forgive me." The nurse said he got weaker so she wheeled him back to his room without him having his cigarette. After the nurse shared with me, I knew then why I felt the peace when I heard Buddy had died. God is so good. He gave me confirmation and my brother was at rest with Him even though he came in the last hour of the day. My brother Willie spoke at Buddy's funeral about Matthew 20: No matter what time of the day the worker came to the vineyard, they all received the same reward: a penny.

THE FOURTH VERSE OF SONG: Now when I had awakened, the tears were in my eyes, and looking all around me and there to my surprise, it was my loving baby. I knew it was a dream and down beside that bed of mine, you should have heard me scream. FATHER WHO ART IN GLORY! I KNOW THY GAVE THINE ONLY SON! FATHER OH PLEASE FORGIVE ME! FOR I WANT TO BE READY WHEN YOU COME!

THANK YOU, LORD JESUS, FOR YOUR SAVING GRACE.

The night I got saved. Have <u>Thine Own Way</u> was the song. I asked Jesus to live in my heart and let His light shine in me! Jesus forgave me of all my sins to remember them no more.

CHAPTER FOUR

"IN BETWEEN TIME"

I will explain my walk with the Lord from age thirteen to thirty. The Lord has always been good to me. If I failed, He would forgive and show me a correct way. If things happened in my life that I couldn't understand, He was there to give me victory over it. I love Him with fear and happiness. I know He will chasten the ones that are His. I loved my mother dearly, but I knew she would straighten me out in a second. You see, this book is not really about me but God. If I wrote about my life only and all the prayers that were answered, it would be a very long book. Some of you reading know the AWESOME GOD we serve and some don't. I felt led to only write about certain highlights in my life to encourage others. There was never a time that I spent without my Heavenly Father. I went through school with friends but not close ones. The telephone we had when I was around fourteen was a party line. We had four families on one line. It was hard to talk to friends or use it very often. My life as a teenager was a lot different from today so I kept my heart and mind on the Lord Jesus. I do believe no matter what times were, my heart would be His. He has been with me my whole life. Even today with my grandchildren, I am deeply concerned about how many things keeps them from knowing my best friend Jesus. Even though some have already accepted the Lord Jesus, I don't see the hunger. The lack of hunger concerns me deeply. I am so thankful that I know the One that can give them the hunger. "BLESSED ARE THEY WHICH DO HUNGER AND THIRST AFTER RIGHTEOUSNESS: FOR THEY SHALL BE FILLED"

I graduated from high school with some honors in 1969. I won a $2,000 scholarship. I knew my parents could not afford to send me to college, so I asked school officials to give the money to someone else. When I was in the eleventh and twelfth grades, I had a part-time job after school, at a furniture store. I had taken shorthand in high school, so I was able to transcribe letters dictated by my manager and type them for him to sign. Accounts receivable was my job also. This was the beginning of my bookkeeping career. You see, I didn't go to college, but

God open doors for me. I knew it was Him. I left the furniture store and went to work for an auto dealership full-time in 1970. At this job I also transcribed letters for my manager, accounts receivable, typing contracts, and doing cash deposits. I worked at this job for nine years. During employment at the car dealership, I was married and had three wonderful little girls. This was over a period of time, of course. In 1979 after all my girls were born, I went to work part-time so I could be with them. At this job, my boss was a gentleman in every respect. I will always remember his kindness and understanding. When he saw a person devoted to their job, he would give a little raise out of the blue. I worked part-time while my children were in school. They never even knew I worked. I would pick them up from school, then go home for snack and home work. It was important to me to be with my children. Later in life when my girls were older, I did go back to work full time and really became a bookkeeper with all the duties of an accountant (payroll, W2's., quarterlies, sales tax, coding, profit and loss statements, accounts payable, accounts receivable, and bank reconciliation for five accounts). My manager even had it to where I could sign checks. Yes, even his and my paycheck had my signature. Isn't God good? He did this for me with all qualifications. After two of my girls were married and having my grandchildren, I became a manager at a big department store. I had responsibilities that God had prepared me for through each and every job. There were eight employees under my supervision. This was what I wanted to go to college for in business management and accounting, but God did it for me. I praise His holy name.

I met Sammy Joe at a church function in 1968. It was a hayride for the youth. He was in the Navy and came home on a weekend leave. He was a blind date set for me. We had a wonderful time on the hayride. Sammy had to leave the next morning to go overseas on a destroyer. I did not see him again until a year later. In the meanwhile our youth class at church sent him some cookies. He did write and tell us he enjoyed the cookies. He said by the time he got the cookies they were like crumbs but he ate every crumb. Then one day I received a personal letter from Sammy. I was glad to hear from him. We continued to write back and forth for a year.

My BIG SURPRISE: One Sunday night as we were having training union, I heard the door open and turned and looked. It was Sammy Joe. The first thing that caught my eyes were his beautiful blue eyes. I almost thought I could swim in them. He looked so handsome. He was dressed in his dark navy blues and his white hat. I have had a few suitors in my time, but I never felt the rush I felt when I saw him standing in the doorway. I smiled and he smiled. After church he gave me a ride home, and I enjoyed his company very much. It was a few months later he was discharged from the navy, and we started dating. Sammy Joe got a job at International Paper Company container division. Even though he worked shift work, he still managed to come see me. After about three months of dating, we were talking one night and he said, "Do you remember when I came to church that night and you turned around and smiled at me?" I said, "yes!" He said, "That's when I fell in love with you." I said to him, "That was the same night I fell in love with you!!!" I know God had a plan when He sent Sammy Joe to me. I had always prayed for the right one in my life. It was like when I saw Sammy that night in church, I knew without a doubt he was the one. We were married July 2, 1971. Thank You, Lord Jesus, for sending me my mate!

I knew I wanted children, and I trusted the Lord in this. I would pray, Lord, you know I want children, but only if they will serve

You. Please don't let them be born if they're going to serve the devil. I meant this with all my heart. Shortly after each child was born, Sammy and I dedicated them to the Lord for His Glory, knowing that it was our responsibility to train them in the way of the Lord. Train up a child in the way he should go: and when he is old, he will not depart from it. THIS IS A PROMISE.

OUR FIRST DAUGHTER: Our first little girl, Lisa Josette, was born February 20, 1973. She had a head full of golden hair. She was beautiful. Everywhere we went with her, people stopped us to see her big blue eyes and red hair. Lisa was always a quiet child. You could just see her studying things around her. Lisa accepted the Lord Jesus at the very young age of seven. During an altar call Lisa went up front by herself. I looked around, and she was gone from her seat. In a panic, I looked up and she was at the altar. I learned later she had told the pastor that she had accepted the Lord Jesus in her heart and she wanted to be baptized. On the way home I was speechless. I was hoping she didn't go to the altar because others went. I really wanted her to know the Lord in a real and mighty way and not just go through the actions. A few days later I talked to our pastor and asked him if he thought she was old enough. He told me he had known other children accepting Jesus at a young age. He also told me when the baptism would be. Boy, I was really concerned. I went to Lisa and asked her, "Do you know what it means to be saved?" She said, "Yes, Momma, I asked Jesus to come live in my heart." She also said, "He died on the cross for me and arose for me." I became speechless again. The Saturday night before her baptism, I went to Lisa's bedroom to pray over her as I did for all my children. I prayed, "Lord Jesus, please let this be real in her life. I don't want her growing up thinking she is saved and is not." I started to leave the room, but I turned around and went back to her bed. I shook her a little and she cracked open her eyes. She said, "What's wrong, Momma?" I said, "I don't want to disturb you, but I need to know if you understand what it means to be baptized." She said, "Yes, Momma. When I go under the water, my old sins will be washed away, and I will come up new. It's just like Jesus dying on the cross and he arose the third day." I was speechless again. We went to church the next morning and Lisa was baptized. I guess I'm a little hard headed or something. I was still concerned about her experience. In my heart it had to be real. Two months later when Sammy and I went to the grocery store near our house, I stayed in the truck with the children. Lisa looked over at me and said, "Momma, did you know we are sisters?" I said with my voice raised, "I'm not your sister; I'm your momma." She said to me again in a calm voice, "But in Christ Jesus we are sisters." I felt so small that I started to weep inside as I answered her. "You're right, honey, we are sisters in Christ Jesus." I never question her salvation again. The Lord taught me a lesson through this experience with my child. I thank Him so much for caring enough to ease my heart. The Lord Jesus assured me that He called her to repentance. How would a seven-year-old know this information? Only from God!!!

Lisa loves the Lord and is always willing to help with different projects in the church. Lisa went to college, and she now is a secondary teacher of math. I would like to share a couple of events that thrilled my heart about her actions during her college life.

Lisa had a conversation with me about how she had seen students in college that claimed to be Christians but partied and drank. She said, "Momma, I think we are the only family that truly believes in God and lives for Him." I said, "No, honey,

God has his remnant everywhere. You really need to pray for those who think they are okay warming a pew and not giving their whole heart to the Lord."

Even when my children were smaller, I would see other children (teenagers) be ashamed of their parents. These other children's parents would just laugh at how they were treated. This bothered me!!! I would pray, please Lord show me how I can be an example where my girls will not be ashamed of me. Another situation that occurred during her college days was a question she asked that I hoped I would never be asked. Lisa called on the phone and said, "Mom, we are on spring break next week, and some of the girls are staying in a family owned beach house for a few days at Surfside. They really want me to go with them. Please can I go?" I was silent for a few seconds before I told her I didn't think this would be right for her. Lisa said, "I didn't think you would let me go, but I thought I would ask because I really wanted to go." I said, "Lisa, you know how to behave----yes, Momma-----I know you are old enough, but I still worry." Lisa said, "Momma, it is a good group of girls I hang around with. I would not have asked if I felt wrong about it." I told her, "You can go, but how long will you stay?" She said,

"Only two days." I asked," Lisa, is there anything you need?" She said, "I could use more clothes." We lived only 30 minutes from Surfside so I said immediately, "I can bring you some clothes." "Oh, Momma, if you could, that would be great!" After she gave me directions, I packed her outfits she asked for and went on my merry way. I suddenly thought oh, I hope Lisa doesn't get embarrassed of me in front of her friends. This was the first time I was faced with the thought of how other children acted to their parents. As I drove up to the beach house, Lisa and one of her friends ran to greet me. Lisa introduced me to her friend and said to me, "Come in, Momma." I said, "No, I do not want to intrude." "Momma, you will not intruding. I want to show you the beach house. It is so big. Wait till you see it." I went in, and her friends were so kind and chatty. The house belonged to one of the girl's parents and it really was clean, big, and had nice furniture. As I was driving home, I started to cry. Lord Jesus You did it again; You answered my prayers I prayed a long time ago. My child was not ashamed of me. THANK YOU, LORD JESUS.

After Lisa graduated from college and began her teaching career, she was married to a special man that came all the way from Connecticut. This is another story in itself that I believe

God ordained. His name is Wayne Sherwood Archer. Wayne and Lisa have given Sammy and me four beautiful grandchildren: Jacob Wayne, Sarah Josette, Hannah Catherine, and Rebekah Jane.

OUR SECOND DAUGHTER: Our second little girl, Dorothy Karen, was born January 25, 1976. Karen was born with dark brown hair (soft curls) and dark blue eyes. She too was a beautiful baby. I had problems with my pregnancy before Karen was born. I went into labor in my eighth month and almost lost her. I really wanted my child, but I remembered my prayer. I knew God would take care of me and her. If the Good Lord Jesus saw fit to take her, I understood. I was bedridden a month before she was born. Thank God He did allow Karen to be born. She was the smallest baby I delivered. Unlike Lisa's quietness, Karen became a chatterbox. It was so cute; she would always grab my face with her little hands and turn it to her face if she was talking to me. Even when I was driving the car, she would do this. I would have to say, "Please, Karen, Momma cannot look at you right now." All her little life she would talk and ask all kinds of questions. One day when she was nine years old, she was asking me how could she accept the Lord Jesus Christ as her savior. I said, "Karen, you just have to repent of sin and accept Him in your heart, believing He died on the cross for you and rose on the third day for you." I said, "We can do this right now, if you would like." She said, Yes, Momma, I want to." We were in the dining room of our home, and we both bowed our heads, held hands, and prayed. After the prayer, I told her to wait until she felt the Lord's presence at church to be baptized. When she was thirteen years old, she went to a crusade. The Lord spoke to her heart, and she knew it was time to be baptized. The next Sunday service she went up front to the altar and told the preacher she was saved and wanted to be baptized. Karen is one child that always thanked God for every bite of food she put in her mouth. Even if it was water she was drinking, she would always bow and thank Him. Karen too has walked with the Lord through teenage and adult life.

In the summer of 1994 Karen was getting ready to go to college, but she did not make it there due to circumstances that occurred. I would like to share how God used her to bring a young man to the Lord. Karen never dated much. She met this young man right after she graduated high school at a fast food restaurant. He got her telephone number and called her quite often. She told us who his parents were. I knew them because I went to school with them.

When they started dating, Karen told me she had to pick him up in her car. I said no! She said, "Momma, you don't understand; he cannot drive, he has epilepsy." He came to our home often, and their relationship grew fast. His family would drop him off at our home and he would wait until Karen got off work. He told me one day he wanted to marry her. I asked, "How will you make a living?" He told me his mother was going to take him to Charleston to see if he could get enrolled in the cooking college. He always wanted to be a chef. His mother did take him, and Karen went with them. Karen told me he was so excited. She said, "Momma, I wish you could have seen his face while he was touring the college." I became worried and talked to the Lord often about this situation.

Chris (boyfriend) told Karen he had quit his medicine because it made him violent. He told her that he had almost hurt his mother. Karen did love him and prayed for him often. Chris began to have seizures more often than his body could bear.

Karen asked him to please go back to the doctor and see if there was something else he could take. He told her he had already been operated on, and he showed her pictures where his head had been cut open about two years before he met her. He told her he had already been told that there was not any more the doctors could do.

Chris did tell Karen he would call his doctor and try some new medicine. Chris called Karen and told her his appointment was to be the next Tuesday. By this time my younger brother Willie had been a preacher for a few years. My girls and I went to his church on Fridays often. Chris would go with us. Chris did become a Christian two months after he and Karen met. One Friday night at the end of August, Chris requested prayer about his new medicine he would be starting on Tuesday. During the same service a man (John) stood up and said he felt that someone needed a closer walk with the Lord and this could be their last chance. Chris got up and went to the altar. The next day (Saturday) Willie's church had an outing at the river; Karen, Chris, and Melanie went. Saturday night after a long day of fun, Karen took Chris home. When Karen got back home she called Chris to let him know she got home safe. As she talked to him, she could tell his voice was really slurred. Karen was worried, so she called his mom to tell her how he sounded. His mother told Karen she would go and check on him. Just a few hours later (in the middle of the night) Karen got a phone call from his mother. She told Karen she had to take Chris to the hospital in Georgetown because his seizures became so severe and he was being transported to Charleston as they spoke. Karen was so devastated! We all got dressed and headed to Charleston. When we arrived at MUSC, Chris was already brain dead (This was early Sunday morning.) On Tuesday, against Karen's heart and wishes, the doctors took his life support from him. Chris died, and his organs were donated. You see, Chris had asked for prayer for his new medicine that he would receive Tuesday. I tried to comfort Karen by telling her he got his new medicine. He would never suffer again. Karen did grieve deeply, but God brought her through. At Chris's funeral, Karen got to read a card that he sent her about loving her and thanking her for the Christian walk she lived before him. Even though this was a short (three months) relationship, God did so much, and a life was saved.

Three years later Karen married Charles E. Frantz, who soon after became a preacher of the gospel. Charlie and Karen have blessed Sammy and me with three beautiful grandchildren: Caleb Elijah, Joshua Samuel, and Esther Elisabeth.

Karen has had the blessing of leading one of her own children to the Lord. Karen has had events in her life that only God brought her through. This is another story in itself that she should tell. What an Awesome God we serve!

OUR THIRD DAUGHTER: Our third little girl, Melanie Ann Renee, was born November 25, 1978. Melanie was born on her great grandmother's birthday, so Sammy and I put Ann in her name in memory of Sammy's grandmother. Melanie was born with dark brown hair and blue eyes. She was also a beautiful baby. I have always told her that she was my challenge. I'll share with you a little story from when she was three years old. One day she was misbehaving while I was cooking. I told her to stop. She didn't stop, so I told her I was going to give her a spanking. Melanie responded by coming in the kitchen and poking her little butt in my face. Oh yes, I had to hide my face to keep from laughing, but I did follow through; I stopped what I was doing and took care of her punishment right then and there. She learned fast how she was supposed to act.

Even though she has a strong will of her own at times, she is strongly dedicated to the Lord. Melanie became a Christian at age twelve. One Sunday the preacher was preaching on Matthew 24:, and the Holy Spirit dealt with her heart. Melanie did not go up right then to the altar, but she told me about the sermon on our walk that afternoon. The Lord dealt with her for three days. When we went to church Wednesday night, she went to the altar to give her life to the Lord. Melanie was baptized shortly after.

Melanie loves the Lord and His word so much. You see, she had the hunger and thirsting. After supper, sometimes my girls and I would walk a mile or two before getting ready for bed. Those were precious walks to me. One night it was just Melanie and me walking alone, and she was carrying her Bible with her. Still to this day she loves to walk, carry her Bible, and read as she walks. As we walked, she said, "Momma the devil has tried to tell me I'm not saved." I jumped in and said, "He tries that with most people, but he lies." Melanie said, "Momma, I know that now. I was lying across my bed the other night, crying and asking God please let me really be saved." She said she felt led to open her Bible; it opened to John chapter 10. She said her eyes fell on verse 14: "I am the good shepherd, and know my sheep, and am known of mine." Melanie said, "Momma, I then read the whole chapter. Jesus does know me!" Melanie began crying. I hugged her and said, "Yes, He knows you and every strand of hair on your head." We had many walks with each other, and the Lord was always present.

I could see that God had given Melanie so much wisdom in the word at a very young age. She even told me at age twelve she felt like she could preach. I said, "If this is from God, He will open the door." We were in service one Friday night at my brother Willie's worship, and he mentioned he would like to hear some of the young fellows preach a sermon. I looked at Melanie. I said, "This is your door open to do what God has laid on your heart." Melanie went to her uncle Willie and told him she would like to preach one night. He gave her a date to give her sermon.

The night came for Melanie to give her sermon. Melanie never told me beforehand what she was going to speak on, but it was Luke 15: 1-10. As she started, I was completely amazed. She explained about the one lost sheep being found with great rejoicing. She compared it with how when one gets saved what rejoicing there is in heaven. I can still see her holding her little arms in a cradling position like the Lord holds us in His arms. She said there is Joy in the presence of the angels of God over one sinner that repenteth. What wisdom the Lord gave her at twelve years old.

There is one more thing I would like to share, an awesome answer to prayer. When Melanie was fourteen years old, we were in one of Willie's services, and he mentioned that he had some friends that were going on a mission trip to Ghana, West Africa, and he was going with them. Melanie looked at me in the service and said, "I would love to go." I said, "You are too young." I asked her, "Why would you want to go?" She started to cry and said, "I know the Lord is coming back and I would like to help win souls to Christ." I said, "Melanie, we will talk about this later."

Weeks went by, and she still had it on her heart to go on this mission trip. She pressed me so about going until I went to talk to Willie. He said, "If God impressed upon her heart to go, you should let her go." Willie also said, they had room for one more. Boy, this was hard. I had always been careful who my girls were around and where they went. God gave them to me, and I had to be wise in choices. I prayed, "Lord I know you gave me Melanie, but she really belongs to you. How can I let her go around the world to people I don't know at all? I know she will be with Willie, but it scares me. Lord Jesus, please let me know if this is you or Melanie." I also told the Lord, "I know it would be impossible to meet the ones she will be going to see for two weeks away from home, but I wish I could. Please Lord, if I just could meet them." As I was praying and crying, I could feel sorrow deep in my soul.

At one of the church services, Willie said he was going to Tennessee for a conference, where representatives come from all over the world to have missionaries go to their country with help. Willie and a committee did go to Tennessee, but they didn't see their contact person. A few hours later Willie met a representative from Ghana. This bishop from Ghana did not see his contact. The bishop and Willie talked for a while and became friends right off from the start. Willie could see the love of Jesus in his heart. The surprising thing was Willie called his wife and said the bishop and his friend would like to come visit our church in Georgetown. Willie said, "I have got to check on their visa and change their air plane tickets. We will be home as soon as this is done." He told his wife what kind of food to buy and prepare. When I heard that the Ghana men were coming to Georgetown, I could hardly believe what I was hearing. First thing I thought I will actually get to meet the ones face to face that my daughter wants to go help with her uncle Willie. Oh, my heart was full; I felt so undeserving but blessed. God did comfort my heart with answered prayer. We do serve an awesome God!!! I knew then that it was meant for Melanie to go. Bishop and his friend were wonderful people. Melanie did go, and she saw people saved, healed, and baptized in the Holy Spirit. Over the years Willie did go back to Africa several times, helping with clothes, toys, Bibles, and he even took a drill to drill water for them. This again is another big story that needs to be told by Willie.

Melanie has had a hunger for the Lord through her teens and adult life. Melanie did go to college. She works for a hospital. Melanie is engaged to a special young man that returned back in her life after twelve years. This was a miracle, with a big story of its own.

Thank you, Lord Jesus, for all three of my girls knowing you in a real and mighty way. My girls' spiritual birth is the greatest gift to them. THANK YOU, LORD JESUS, FOR YOUR SAVING GRACE.

Our Wedding-July 2, 1971

Our girls: Lisa, Karen and Melanie

Melanie at age 14 in Africa with her Uncle Willie.

Sammy Joe and I sitting in my prayer swing.

Our family 2010

CHAPTER FIVE

THIRTY YEARS OLD

This was a growing time for me. You are never too old to learn. Being a child of God, you are always learning. Most of all, we need to learn to lean on Him.

On February 26, 1980, I turned thirty years old. All day long I was weeping and could not stop. I know sometimes when I was weeping that was prayer time for something that was about to happen, and I would be prayed up to handle it or help others around me. This day of my birthday was different. All day long I was asking God for strength, begging Him to forgive me for not doing more for Him. I even wanted to be a better mother and wife. I will share how He answered my prayer a little later in this chapter. But first I need to tell you something that really did happen on my birthday that affected a lot of people.

My sister Hannah died August 13, 1972. She was only thirty-four years old. She left behind five children. My mother continued raising four of them, ages fifteen to seven years of age. Hannah's youngest son was seven years old at the time of her death. Eight years later this is the one who had a bad accident on my birthday in 1980 at 5:30 PM. He was fifteen years old at the time. He was riding on the front of a go-cart backwards position while two other boys were in the seat. A man was plowing a garden and drove the tractor in the road to turn around. The boys ran into the disc that was attached to the tractor, and my nephew's head was cut open. He was rushed to MUSC, and doctors induced a coma. Days later the doctors said he appeared to be brain dead and they wanted to take the life support off him. Mother said no! You see, Momma was a woman of faith. She knew what God could do. This is really a story in itself, and I will shorten it to tell you he did come out of the coma within four months. He was like a vegetable at first. He had to be tied in his wheel chair. By the grace of God he did learn to talk and walk again. Years later his memory did come back.

I needed to tell you the above to set what happened the first week he was in the hospital. My sister Joyce came from Alabama to help Momma at home and at the hospital. Joyce came to my house before going to Charleston. We had a big snow that week in February, so she decided to stay the night with me until the weather cleared up.

After Sammy and the girls went to bed, it gave us time to talk. I shared with Joyce how I felt so weak at times in the Spirit. I would get up to sing in church, and I even felt weak in my knees. I told her I really didn't understand because I know that Jesus is my Savior, best friend, and He is with me. She said, "Dot, I don't know what is wrong but God does. Why don't we read the Bible and say a prayer and maybe God will reveal to you what is wrong?" I said, "That sounds like a good idea." I got my Bible and sat down by Joyce on the sofa. She said, "Why don't you read something first?" I told her, "Nothing comes to mind right now, but sometimes I just open His Word and He gives me an answer." She said, "Well, just open the Bible." I opened the Bible to Matthew 6, and my eyes fell on verse 14: "For if ye forgive men their trespasses, your heavenly Father will also forgive you: 15 But if ye forgive not men their trespasses, neither will your Father forgive your trespasses." As I read verse 15, I stopped and started it over again; it's like the words just jumped right off the page to my face. I looked up at Joyce and said, "Could it be unforgiveness?" Joyce said, "Yes, not forgiving can destroy people, even ones that love the Lord, and their joy can be robbed also." I did not realize that I had been harboring so much in my heart. Joyce and I began to pray; I was praying out loud. As I prayed, I saw so many faces and the things that they had done to me. Every face I saw I said, Lord I forgive them; please forgive me for holding this in my heart. Believe me, the prayer was a lengthy one. I had no idea I had all that sin in me. It was unbelievable, but it really happened. In the prayer, each time I would ask God to forgive me, my heart was lighter. I told Joyce I felt so much better. Joy was overflowing out of me! Joyce and I stayed up a little longer; then she decided to go to bed. I said, "It is late; it's almost 2 AM." Joyce went on to bed and so did I, but I could not go to sleep. I got up and went to the kitchen. I told the Lord I felt so happy. I started twirling around in the kitchen. I told the Lord I felt so free. I felt like a bird let out of a cage. I heard Him say through my being, "Dot, I was there all the time." The conversation was so real to me that I answered, "Yes, You were."

I knew I had heard a song "He Was There All the Time." I said, "Lord, if the song is real, please let me find it." I did find the song with the help of my pastor's wife. This is a another song that is dear to my heart, which I love to sing.

When things are said and done to hurt me, I immediately turn them over to the Lord. My heart's desire is to be close to Jesus and not allow anything or anyone to come between. Thank You, Lord, for being there all the time!!!

On my thirtieth birthday, I also asked God to make me be the best mother and wife. At the ages of thirty and thirty-one, God showed me so much through His word. I would like to share an event that led up to the hunger to search His word.

On Saturdays I worked part time and got off at 1 PM. Sammy would be home with our girls; it was seldom for him to work on Saturdays. When he did work, my mother cared for our children. As I went to work, I left responsibilities for the two older girls to put folded clothes in their dresser drawers and Sammy to clean dishes after he fed the girls breakfast, so I could cook when I came home. I wasn't feeling too well that day. I came home after work, opened the front door, saw Sammy rocking Melanie in the rocking chair and the other two girls sitting on the floor in front of the television. All four of them were laughing at the television show and enjoying each other. Instead of me laughing with them, I got angry as I looked around and saw the clothes still in the chair. I said hello to my family and walked to the kitchen. I just got in a selfish mode and thought to myself "Am I a slave?" Well, God really taught me a lesson.

I didn't say anything about them not following through; I just started banging pots as I started to prepare food. All of a sudden I heard Melanie crying. Lisa and Karen were arguing going down the hall taking their clothes to their rooms. I looked out the kitchen window and I saw Sammy walking back and forth under the big oak tree talking to himself. Tears came to my eyes and my heart just broke. Oh Lord Jesus, what did I do? My family was laughing and being happy. I came in, and now everyone is upset. The Lord did quicken me; I did feel guilty about acting angry and banging pots. He said through my being, "You can make or break this home." I said, "I can make or break this home." I prayed, Lord Jesus, please teach me, show me how I can be the best mom and wife. I looked again at Sammy through the window and just cried. I loved him and I felt so bad for upsetting him.

Days and even months went by, and God was dealing with me and showing me so much in His word. We had a swing in the back yard between two trees. This became my prayer closet. When Sammy was working evening shift and the girls were in bed, the Lord and I were in the swing. As I prayed, He would show me things that I was handling wrong. I would just cry and say, "Lord, I didn't realize. Please show me."

First of all, as a wife and mother, I am not a slave. It is my duty to love, raise my children, and be a help mate to my husband. There were many things God showed me, but I would like to share a couple of events. Scriptures He gave me will be at the end of the chapter.

Children: I had always made sure that I monitored TV shows they watched, careful who their company was, took them to church, taught them about the Lord and His Love. I never lied to them. If I promised them a treat or a spanking, I always followed through. I felt there was more that I could do for the children, and I wanted the Lord's anointing to do so. God showed me how.

One day Melanie came to me in the kitchen, while I was cooking. She wanted to tell me something, and I said wait a minute. The Holy Spirit quickened me so fast that I said, "Melanie, come back sweetheart." I took my boiling pot off the burner, set it aside, and said to Melanie, "What did you have to tell Momma?" She began to tell me; it was not a big thing, but it was big to her. I helped her and she went on her merry way. It only took a few minutes to answer her and she was happy. My dinner was not late and I felt happy inside. It was the little things I was missing that made big happy endings. From then on if my girls needed me, I quit what I was doing and helped them. I have always loved being a mother. When I let self go, I was blessed. Psalms 128: 3 "Thy wife shall be as a fruitful vine by the sides of thine house: Thy children like olive plants roundabout thy table." My girls and I are really close then and now. They each have told me at different times, "You are my best friend."

HUSBAND: As I sat in my prayer swing, the Lord showed me how selfish I was as I pondered the scriptures I had read. I would cry as I prayed and asked for wisdom. The Lord took me back to when our first child Lisa was a baby. Sammy would come home from work. He would come in and give me a kiss and say, "How was your day?" Boy, I would start my woe is me: tell him what a hard day I had, not ask him about his day until hours later. This particular day Lisa was sick. I told him Lisa was cutting teeth, she had fever, and she would not sleep when I laid her down. I'd had to hold her all day. He told me, "Give her to me." He would put her on his big, strong shoulder, hum a little, and I could see her dozing off to sleep. I asked him, "How did you do that? She wouldn't go to sleep for me. Please lay her down and come eat." The Lord showed me this because Sammy worked a lot harder than I. He was on a cement floor for eight or sometimes sixteen hours, came home, helped me, and never complained. Boy, did I cry when I realized how selfish I had been. It was like the unforgiveness that I experienced. The Lord was truly doing a purging in me. I thanked Him for showing me. I got up out of the swing, went inside, and starting cleaning my house.

I used to get upset when I would see Sammy's bath tub ring in the tub. He did work hard, and he came home really dirty. As I started cleaning the ring in the tub, I started thanking God that I had a wonderful husband to take care of me. As I went through the house picking up his clothes and shoes, I was thanking God again and again for his blessing for having a husband that loved and took care of me.

Sammy was on evening shift that day. When he came home, he came home to a different wife. I have always loved him, but God showed me how to love him. After I put the children to bed, I took a shower, put on makeup at 10:30 PM, curled my hair a little, and fixed him a hot meal. As he walked through the front door, I came from the kitchen to meet him. I gave him a big hug and welcome home kiss. He said, "Wow! you look beautiful." I said, "Thank you. How was your day?" He said, "My day was nothing like this; let's just enjoy each other." I told him, "I have hot food ready for you." He said, "I'll eat later I like looking at what is before me."

When I changed, there was a big change in Sammy. I never had to ask him to help anymore. He did things for me around the house without asking him. He even put his clothes in the clothes hamper, and I never told him to. I learned that even in a marriage, children, self has to die just like being a Christian. Sammy was thoughtful and still is even after forty-two years of marriage. We still feel like newlyweds. Thank You, Lord Jesus, for showing me how to love.

SCRIPTURES: Genesis 2:15 And the Lord God took the man, and put him into the garden of Eden to dress it and to keep it.

2:16 And the Lord God commanded the man, saying, Of every tree of the garden thou mayest freely eat:

2:17 But the tree of the knowledge of good and evil, thou shalt not eat of it: for in the day that thou eatest thereof thou shalt surely die.

2:18 And the Lord God said, It is not good that the man should be alone; I will make him an help meet for him.

2:21 And the Lord God caused a deep sleep to fall upon Adam, and he slept; and He took one of his ribs, and closed up the flesh instead thereof:

2:22 And the rib, which the Lord God had taken from man, made He a woman, and brought her unto the man.

2:23 And Adam said, this is now bone of my bones, and flesh of my flesh: she shall be called woman, because she was taken out of man.

2:24 Therefore shall a man leave his father and his mother and shall cleave unto his wife: and they shall be one flesh.

2:25 And they were both naked, the man and his wife, and were not ashamed.

3:1 Now the serpent was more subtle than any beast of the field which the Lord God had made. And he said unto the woman, Yea hath God said, Ye shall not eat of every tree of the garden?

3:2 And the woman said unto the serpent, We may eat of the fruit of the trees of the garden:

3:3 But of the fruit of the tree which is in the midst of the garden, God hath said, Ye shall not eat of it neither shall ye touch it, lest ye die.

3:4 And the serpent said unto the woman, Ye shall not surely die:

3:5 For God doth know that in the day ye eat thereof, then your eyes shall be opened, and ye shall be as gods, knowing good and evil.

3:6 And when the woman saw that the tree was good for food, and that it was pleasant to the eyes, and a tree to be desired to make one wise, she took of the fruit thereof, and did eat, and gave also unto her husband with her; and he did eat.

3:7 And the eyes of them both were opened, and they knew that they were naked; and they sewed fig leaves together, and made themselves aprons.

3:8 And they heard the voice of the Lord God walking in the garden in the cool of the day: and Adam and his wife hid themselves from the presence of the Lord God amongst the trees of the garden.

3:9 And the Lord God called unto Adam, and said unto him, Where art thou?

3:10 And he said, I heard thy voice in the garden, and I was afraid, because I was naked; and I hid myself.

3:11 And he said, Who told thee that thou wast naked? Hast thou eaten of the tree, whereof I commanded thee that thou shouldest not eat?

3:12 And the man said, The woman whom thou gavest to be with me, she gave me of the tree, and I did eat.

3:13 And the Lord God said unto the woman, What is this that thou hast done? And the woman said, The serpent beguiled me, and I did eat.

What Happens When We are Disobedient

3:14 And the Lord God said unto the serpent, Because thou hast done this, thou art cursed above all cattle, and above every beast of the field; upon thy belly shalt thou go, and dust shalt thou eat all the days of thy life:

3:15 And I will put enmity between thee and the woman, and between thy seed and her seed; it shall bruise thy head, and thou shalt bruise his heel.

3:16 Unto the woman he said, I will greatly multiply thy sorrow and thy conception; in sorrow thou shalt bring forth children; and thy desire shall be to thy husband, and he shall rule over thee.

3:17 And unto Adam he said, Because thou hast hearkened Unto the voice of thy wife, and hast eaten of the tree, of which I commanded thee, saying, Thou shalt not eat of it: cursed is the ground for thy sake; in sorrow shalt thou eat of it all the days of thy life;

3:18 Thorns also and thistles shall it bring forth to thee; and thou shalt eat the herb of the field;

3:19 In the sweat of thy face shalt thou eat bread, till thou return unto the ground; for out of it wast thou taken: for dust thou art, and unto dust shalt thou return.

Dorothy L. Cunningham

Wives Are the Weaker Vessel

I Peter 3:7 Likewise, ye husbands dwell with them according to knowledge, giving honour unto the wife, as unto the weaker vessel, and as being heirs together of the grace of life; that your prayers be not hindered.

A Woman in Anger

Proverbs 21:19 It is better to dwell in the wilderness, than with a contentious and an angry woman.

Duties to Our Husbands

Ephesians 5:22 Wives, submit yourselves unto your own Husbands, as unto the Lord.

5:23 For the husband is the head of the wife, even as Christ is the head of the church; and He is the savior of the body.

Proverbs 12:4 A virtuous woman is a crown to her husband: but she that maketh ashamed is rottenness in his bones.

Proverbs 31:10 Who can find a virtuous woman? for her price is far above rubies.

31:11 The heart of her husband doth safely trust in her, so that he shall have no need of spoil.

31:12 She will do him good and not evil all the days of her life.

<u>Husbands Can Be Won to the Lord</u>
<u>by the Conversation of the Wife</u>

I Peter 3:1 Likewise ye wives, be in subjection to your own husbands; that, if any obey not the word, they, also may without the word be won by the conversation of the wives:

3:2 While they behold your chaste conversation coupled with fear.

Mothers Over the Home

I Timothy 5:14 I will therefore that the younger women marry, bear children, guide the house, give none occasion to the adversary to speak reproachfully.

Titus 2:3 The aged women likewise, that they be in behavior as becometh holiness, not false accusers, not given to much wine, teachers of good things:

2:4 That they may teach the young women to be sober (wise), to love their husbands, to love their children:

2:5 To be discreet (intelligent), chaste (consecrated pure), keepers at home, good, obedient to their own husbands, that the word of God be not blasphemed.

Proverbs 31:27 She looketh well to the ways of her household, and eateth not the bread of idleness.

Psalms 128:3 Thy wife shall be as a fruitful vine by the sides of thine house: Thy children like olive plants round about thy table.

<u>Guiding Our Children</u>

Proverbs 6:2 Thou art snared with the words of thy mouth, thou art taken with the words of thy mouth.

Proverbs 22:6 Train up a child in the way he should go: and when he is old, he will not depart from it.

Proverbs 22:15 Foolishness is bound in the heart of a child; but the rod of correction shall drive it far from him.

I Timothy 3:4 One that ruleth well his own house, having his children in subjection with all gravity:

Colossians 3:21 Fathers, provoke not your children to anger, lest they be discouraged.

Ephesians 6:4 And, ye Fathers, provoke not your children to wrath; but bring them up in the nurture and admonitions of the Lord.

Deuteronomy 6:4 Hear O Israel: The Lord our God is one Lord:

6:5 And thou shalt love the Lord thy God with all thine heart, and with all thy soul, and with all thy might.

6:6 And these words which I command thee this day shall be in thine heart:

6:7 And thou shalt teach them diligently unto thy children, and shalt talk of them when thou sittest in thine house, and when thou walkest by the way, and when thou liest down, and when thou risest up.

Joshua 24:15 And if it seem evil unto you to serve the Lord, choose you this day whom ye will serve, whether the gods which your fathers served that were on the other side of the flood, or the gods of the Amorites in whose land ye dwell: but as for me and my house, we will serve the Lord.

Weeping for Our Children

Luke 23:28 But Jesus turning unto them said Daughters of Jerusalem, weep not for me, but weep for yourselves, and for your children.

Jeremiah 31:15 Thus saith the Lord, A voice was heard in Ramah, lamentation (mourning), and bitter weeping: Rahel weeping for her children refused to be comforted for her children, because they were not.

31:16 Thus saith the Lord; Refrain thy voice from weeping, and thine eyes from tears: for thy work shall be rewarded, saith the Lord: and they shall come again from the land of the enemy.

31:17 And there is hope in thine end, saith the Lord, that thy children shall come again to their own border.

Scriptures to Share with Our Children

Ephesians 6:1 Children, obey your parents in the Lord: for this is right.

6:2 Honor thy Father and Mother; which is the first commandment with promise;

6:3 That it may be well with thee, and thou mayest live long on the earth.

John 3:16 For God so loved the world, that he gave his only begotten Son, that whosoever believeth in him should not perish, but have everlasting life.

Romans 10:9 That if thou shalt confess with thy mouth the Lord Jesus, and shalt believe in thine heart that God hath raised him from the dead, thou shalt be saved.

10:10 For with the heart man believeth unto righteousness: and with the mouth confession is made unto salvation.

10:13 For whosoever shall call upon the name of the Lord shall be saved.

10:17 So then faith cometh by hearing, and hearing by the word of God.

Jeremiah 23:23 Am I a God at hand, saith the lord, and not a God afar off?

23:24 Can any hide himself in secret places that I shall not see him? saith the Lord. Do not I fill heaven and earth? saith the Lord.

Psalm 11:4 The Lord is in his holy temple, the Lord's throne is in heaven: his eyes behold, his eyelids try, the children of men.

Hebrews 4:13 Neither is there any creature that is not manifest in his sight: but all things are naked and opened unto the eyes of him with whom we have to do.

4:14 Seeing then that we have a great high priest, that is passed into the heavens, Jesus the Son of God, let us hold fast our profession.

4:15 For we have not an high priest which cannot be touched with the feeling of our infirmities; but was in all points tempted like as we are. yet without sin.

I Corinthians 6:18 Flee fornication. Every sin that a man doeth is without the body; but he that committeth fornication sinneth against his own body.

10:13 There hath no temptation taken you but such as is common to man: but God is faithful, who will not suffer you to be tempted above that ye are able; but will with the temptation also make a way to escape, that ye may be able to bear it.

James 1:13 Let no man say when he is tempted, I am tempted of God: for God cannot be tempted with evil, neither tempteth he any man:

1:14 But every man is tempted, when he is drawn away of his own lust, and enticed.

Generation to Generation

II Timothy 1:5 When I call to remembrance the unfeigned faith that is in thee, which dwelt first in thy grandmother Lois, and thy mother Eunice, and I am persuaded that in thee also.

THANK YOU, LORD JESUS, FOR YOUR LIVING WORD.

CHAPTER SIX

THIRTY-ONE YEARS OLD

This was a time in my life, I never knew what I was about to experience, but the Lord God had prepared me for it. The previous chapter when I turned thirty set the stage, by Him purging me so.

I would like to go back in time and share a conversation my mother and I had when I was a teen. One day when I was sitting at the dining table with Momma, I was thinking about my future of being married someday. I told Momma, "When I get married, I'm going to treat my mother-in-law really special, like I treat you, Momma, because she will be my husband's mother." Momma told me that was an excellent idea; mothers should be respected no matter whose mother.

When it came my time in life to marry, that is when my whole life changed. Sammy and I dated three and a half years before we were married. I was twenty-one years old, and Sammy was twenty-six years old when we were married.

His mother liked me at first until he gave me a ring; then she changed. He was her baby, and I always tried to attribute her actions to that thought. When it got closer to our wedding date, she got worse. I won't share the hurtful things out of respect for her.

My sister Marie, from Virginia, came home to help Momma and me with the wedding. I was so hurt by remarks from my future mother-in-law until I was in tears most of the time. On the eve of my wedding day, Marie told me that she would take me to Virginia that night if I didn't want to go through with the wedding. I thought maybe I shouldn't marry Sammy, but I knew he was the one for me. I truly loved him. Through the tears, my heart lifted up, and I told Marie, "He needs me, and I love him. If I don't marry him, he'll never have a life." I do believe the good Lord gave me that thought. It carried me through for a long time.

This was when I started holding things in my heart. An unforgiving nature crept upon me. I had never in my life experienced the feeling of someone not liking me. I just did not understand the rejection from her. She would never give me a chance to treat her like my heart wanted to, as I had told my mother I would.

God gave me the chance though. God allowed me to go through nine years of this rejection until He was ready. When I was thirty years old, he freed me from so much hurt because I had something I had to do that would take a clean, pure heart to do it.

After Sammy's father passed, his mother lived alone. She did alright for awhile, but her health got worse. She didn't see very well due to diabetes. I don't think she was eating right. She needed someone to care for her. One of her sons and his family moved in for a while, but it didn't work out. They left her. A little while later the same son and family moved in again. It didn't work the second time. There was talk among her children to put her in a nursing home.

Sammy was devastated; he did not want his mother in a nursing home. One day when Sammy came out of the bathroom, he was crying. I could see tears on his face. I had never really seen Sammy cry before. I told him I would help him in any way that I could to care for his mother. I told him to call her and see if she would come stay with us. I told him I would make room for her. We both called and talked to her, but she would not agree to come to our home. She told us that she was staying right there at her own home, even if she had to stay by herself.

Sammy went to work after the phone call. Later that day Mrs. Cunningham called and asked if we would go stay with her. I was totally shocked. I told her I would talk to Sammy and see how we could work it. I called Sammy at work and told him his mother had called back and wanted us to go to her home.

This was a big step. Two of our children were in school and would have to change schools. Our youngest daughter Melanie was almost three. I would have to quit my part-time job to care for Mrs. Cunningham and my family properly. I was worried about quitting my job because at the time in 1981 Sammy's job was cut to four days a week most all that year.

Sammy and I went to the Lord in prayer. Somehow we felt God would work it all out for us and his mom. Even though circumstances looked bleak, God gave us peace to try. We went to her home, for a while living out of a suit case.

Sammy and I had to make a decision to sink or swim. By faith we took the plunge and moved our girls to a school in his parents' neighborhood. It became hard to make our house payment since I had quit my job. Sammy's work was still only four days a week. We felt led to rent our house out while we were helping his mother. It happened so fast; it wasn't hard to rent at all. A nice young couple from up north had transferred to Georgetown due to work. They read our ad in the paper and wanted to rent our home. We told them we would have to rent year by year because we weren't sure when we would be coming back home due to our circumstances. They agreed to the contract. Sammy and I were at peace knowing that God had taken care of our home for us.

To get back to Mrs. Cunningham, she had to be fed three meals and three snacks a day due to her diabetes. I had never given anyone shots before, but God made it easy for me. It's almost like He gave me wisdom right on the spot. I had to give her two shots a day. I remember her telling me one time that I was so tender giving her shots that she hardly felt it. This was so helpful to my spirit. You see, she didn't stop saying harsh things to me, but I was so busy taking care of her, Sammy, and the girls that it didn't matter what she said. I took care of her no matter what. I had a drive that only God gave me. I was at peace. When God is on the scene, there is peace. He showed me that I loved Mrs. Cunningham no matter if she never loved me.

There were even times I felt a guardian angel was helping me. For instance, I was helping her to the bathroom, and she sat right down on the floor in the hall before entering the bathroom. I said, "Oh!! Mrs. Cunningham, please don't do this; we are almost there." "I'm too weak," she said. I was alone helping her: Sammy was at work, the girls in school, and Melanie was too small. I said, "Lord, please help me." It was like I had strength that came out of nowhere. I was only 124 pounds at the time, but I lifted her back to her feet without hurting her. The Lord knew that I was mostly worried about pulling on her and hurting her. As we walked in the bathroom, I was thanking God out loud for His help and the guardian angel He sent me.

After a year or more Mrs. Cunningham seemed to be doing better; her sugar readings were looking better. She even rode off with us on one occasion to get ice cream. She wanted some ice cream, so I didn't think it would hurt since her sugar levels were low. Not often, but we did have little happy times. She still at any chance she had would try to pull me down. Mrs. Cunningham would get on the phone with her friend and speak out loud about what people were saying about Sammy and me staying with her to get what she had. I was making up the beds that day when I heard this and I just fell across the bed and wept. I said, "Lord Jesus, doesn't she realize we love her and we gave up our home life to share with her?"

In the latter part of the second year, Mrs. Cunningham began to go down in health again. She would have a hard time sleeping because she said her shoulders hurt so bad. At night I would rub her shoulders with Ben-Gay. At first the rub was enough, but then later she would ask for Sammy or me to lie down with her till she fell asleep. Sammy had to work shift work, so it turned out that I was the one to lie with her till she fell off to sleep most of the time. Weeks turned into months and I was barely getting any sleep at all. Mrs. Cunningham would fall off to sleep, so I would creep out the bed and go to my bed. A few minutes later I would hear D-O-T real loud; I would quickly jump up and go to her before she woke the children. Months of no sleeping made me ill. My eyes were seeing double at times and my head hurt something awful.

A home health nurse started coming in to take her vitals and help me bathe her. The nurse suggested a hospital bed. After she got the hospital bed, it was easier to care for her. I could lift her head up and down. Mrs. Cunningham got to where she could not eat. Sammy and I would try hard to get her to eat. She would eat a little but not much. It was like her throat would not let her swallow. Sammy mostly fed her at the end because I knew it would make her happy having her baby son feed her.

I had to finally go to the doctor about my head. The doctor visit was on a Thursday. The doctor said it looked like Bell's palsy. He told me he was going to make me an appointment in Charleston. The only thing was the Bell's palsy did not strike to go dead; it was very painful. The left side of my head felt really big, but when I looked in the mirror, I looked normal. My gums had risen up off my teeth, and my mouth and eye were turning up. I went to the Lord in prayer about this situation. I read in His word James 5:14-15: "Is any sick among you? let him call for the elders of the church; and let them pray over him, anointing him with oil in the name of the Lord: And the prayer of faith shall save the sick, and the Lord shall raise him up; and it he have committed sins, they shall be forgiven him." This scripture was powerful to me. I told Sammy I must go to my brother's church Sunday and have them anoint me and pray for me. I did go, and I asked for prayer. Frank and the men of his church anointed me with oil and prayed. As they were praying for me, I felt something burst in my head until it made me cry out loud. As I went back to my seat beside my niece, I told her I felt warm oil flowing all over the left side of my head, over my eye, around my ear, through my gums, and down my throat. It was the warmest, most soothing feeling that I had ever experienced. She said, "That's wonderful. I said, "Yes," while in tears of joy. I knew the Lord had healed me. The manifestation did not come right then, but I knew it all the same.

Monday morning came, and Sammy got off work to take me to Charleston to the doctor. I went to Mrs. Cunningham's bedroom to see her before I left, to see if there was something I could do for her. By this time she was not talking much and the words she would say were not plain. I told her Johnny (one of her sons) was coming over to sit with her while we were gone. When I started to the door to leave, she cried out. I went back to her, but she said nothing. I said to her, "Can I get you something or change you?" She said nothing. Again I started out the door, and again she cried out. I went back to her for the third time and said, "What is wrong?" She took her hands, grabbed my left arm, pulled herself up to my left ear, and said, "Dot, I need you." In an instant all those years of hurt just vanished. Those words she spoke just rang through my heart. I knew then she really knew I loved her for her. I also knew she really knew me for who I was. I told her she had me, kissed her on the forehead, and said, "I will be back as soon as the doctor's appointment is over. Well, it did not go as planned. The doctor in Charleston put me in the hospital, which turned into a three-week stay.

Three days after I was in the hospital in Charleston, Mrs. Cunningham had a stroke. Sammy came to me and told me she was in the Georgetown Hospital with a stroke. I thought of her so; I wished I could go see her. I told Sammy to spend as much time with his mother as he could. I already knew his trips to Charleston would be fewer.

I had all kinds of tests run on me. The doctors were baffled at my condition. They could clearly see my paralysis but were not quite clear where it was coming from. I had a spinal tap and all sorts of tests but no answers as yet. The next week on a Wednesday morning I had to have a test where they put dye in the main artery of my right groin that shot up to the left side of my head. Sammy was supposed to be with me for this. When he did not come, I knew something was wrong. I told my doctor that something must have happened to Sammy's mother or he would have been here. Well, later I found out the doctors and nurses already knew about Mrs. Cunningham dying. They would not tell me anything because of my condition. Sammy came later after the procedure and told me his mom had passed away during the same time he was supposed to be with me. I told him I knew something had happened and he did right to be by his mother's bedside.

After I had kissed Mrs. Cunningham's forehead that morning I left, I never knew that would be the last time I would see her. She and I had a blessed ending. GOD IS GOOD.

Sammy Joe loves my help.

CHAPTER SEVEN

THIRTY-THREE YEARS OLD

I had turned thirty-three while we were still living at Mrs. Cunningham's. We lived with and took care of her for almost three years. God showed me so much in those three years. I believe He showed Mrs. Cunningham also. The freedom I felt in my soul was worth all that we went through. My children took everything well; Sammy and I were still close. God is good!!!

When I became thirty-three, I had two events in my life that made me grow even stronger.

HEALING: When I was released from the hospital, I still had the paralysis and I was sent home on several medicines. My heart felt really weak at times. The only thing the doctor could tell me from Charleston was that I had really overworked nerves.

The Lord brought back to my memory the prayer that was prayed over me. I remembered the warm oil flowing in my body. I told the Lord Jesus I knew I was healed but I still had this pain. I knew never to question God; I knew it was in His timing.

I went to my brother Frank's church one Wednesday night shortly after I came home from the hospital. He had a guest speaker that night. He and his wife lived in Louisiana. He was in Georgetown due to his job on a dredge in Winyah Bay. This man was full of faith in God. I listened to him very carefully, and it was like faith rose up in me so strong. I said, "Lord, I know you healed me. Show me."

My daughters and I went home after service. I fed them a snack and off to bed they went. I started to take my medicine and faith rose up in me again. I said, "Lord Jesus, I know You healed me and these medicines might be hindering me." I told the Lord I was finished with this medicine.

The devil said to me in my thoughts: Sammy's working graveyard; what if you die in your sleep? The girls will be alone. I said boldly back, "If I die tonight, it won't be Jesus' fault; it will be mine." One of the medicines had to be tapered off of, but I quit it with the others. The next morning when Sammy came home, I told him what I did. Of course, he seemed worried. I even coughed up blood for two days, but I never lost faith. Sammy kept telling me to take my medicine. In about two weeks I was fine. My face was back to normal, and my gums had relaxed back down on my teeth. I was at peace and healthy again. Thank You, Lord Jesus, for healing me.

BAPTISM IN THE HOLY SPIRIT: During my stay at Mrs. Cunningham's, I began another hunger in my life that I would like to share. Sammy and I would take turns taking the girls to church since one of us had to stay with his mom. One Sunday morning while cooking, as Mrs. Cunningham was napping, I was listening to preaching on TV. The sermon was eye opening to me. The preacher was using Acts 2:38-39 as his text. I opened my Bible to this scripture, and these two verses just jumped off the page at me. I was raised Baptist, but even in all my walk with the Lord I knew inside I lived by His Word and not what a denomination says. I was thirty-two years old and I had not heard this teaching before. I cried out as the Holy Spirit drew me: "Lord, please give me all I need to serve you. Lord, it says plainly in the 39th verse, For the promise is unto you, and to your children, and to all that are afar off, even as many as the Lord our God shall call. I'm afar off; please Lord show me." This sermon stayed with me for a long time and I searched scriptures again as I performed my duties taking care of Sammy's mom and my family.

After Mrs. Cunningham died and I received my healing, I started visiting different types of churches. I was searching for the truth. I would not recommend this to anyone because confusion can arise. I do believe me visiting these different churches prolonged me receiving my Baptism in the Holy Spirit. I will share a few experiences.

I went to a holiness church near where I lived. I felt scared even before I went in because I went alone. I sat down, and singing and shouting started. I felt a coldness instead of warmth. While the preacher was preaching, so many were talking and shouting to where I knew they couldn't hear what he was saying. When I left, I sat in my car, put my head on the steering wheel, and just wept. I said, "Lord Jesus, I could not feel your presence in there. It was cold and scary. I don't understand." A few weeks later, I went to a revival in a nearby town. I was invited by someone I knew, so the entrance to the service was more becoming. I could feel God's presence during the singing and preaching. I went to the altar to talk to the Lord like I had done thousands of times. As I was praying, someone grabbed me and pulled me back to lay on the floor. I knew in my heart they were only trying to help me but I was so startled until it scared me. Different ones were praying over me, but I had no understanding of what had just happened. Again I left a service in weeping, asking God to show me because I could not feel His presence in what just happened. I cried most of the way home, asking God for understanding. As weeks and months went by, I was still searching for answers. I did learn that all are not His. There are counterfeits that hinder the Lord's work, but God does have His remnant.

One warm summer evening in August, I went to visit my younger brother Willie. He had had a wonderful experience at a tent revival, so I wanted to talk to him about what God had done for him. I enjoyed hearing about his touch from the Lord. Hours went by, and before I knew it, his wife and children had already gone to bed. We talked about Daddy, how much he loved the Lord, and his Christian life he lived before us. We talked about Momma, her Christian walk, and how she guided us children. We talked about many scriptures. Our conversation was long and a blessing. Before Willie and I knew it, it was already 2 A.M. I told Willie I needed to go so he could go to bed. Willie said to me, "Dot, let's have prayer before you go. I'll pray for you first and then you pray for me." I said, "That will be great."

I was sitting in a straight back chair, so Willie went behind me and put his hands on my shoulders. Willie starting praying for me and I was praying also with weeping. I said to the Lord Jesus, "I KNOW I LIVE IN THIS WORLD BUT I DON'T WANT TO BE OF THIS WORLD. I ONLY WANT TO BE OF THEE." As soon as the words came out of my mouth, I grew so big that Willie's hands felt like baby hands on my shoulders. My eyes were shut, but the light was so bright until I could see it through my eyelids. My tongue got so thick until I couldn't utter a word. I felt like I was caught up in His Glory. I thought, "GOD, YOU ARE AWESOME." When the prayer was over, Willie said, "Dot, I believe you received a blessing." I said, "I did!" God's power is so AWESOME and GLORIOUS. Willie, I was trying to tell the

Lord to bless you too, but my tongue was thick. This blessing has stayed with me. I will never forget His presence. My heart was ready to receive and I did.

It took me a year to receive the baptism in the Holy Spirit. If you are His child, all you have to do is ask and receive with your heart. I do have a heavenly prayer language in the Holy Spirit that is often spoken. I am bolder about telling others about Christ Jesus and what He did on the cross. From thirty-three years old until now, the Lord and I have walked even a stronger walk, because I KNOW, I KNOW. Thank you, Lord Jesus, for the gift of the baptism in the Holy Spirit.

TO GOD BE THE GLORY!

*All scripture referenced comes from the King James Version of God's Holy Word.